Harry's Homilies

Books by David Ellis

Deus ex Machina Sapiens:
The Emergence of Machine Intelligence

Technology and the Future of Health Care:
Preparing for the Next 30 Years

The Oakwood Trilogy
Compiled & Edited by David Ellis
Volume 1: ? *(Donald W. Weaver*)
Volume 2: Harry's Homilies *(Harry Tompkins)*
Volume 3: Fayth *(Faten Rihani)*

Harry's Homilies
Heart and Soul

compiled and edited
by David Ellis

with a Foreword
by Donald W. Weaver, M.D.

Copyright © 2014 Elysian Detroit

Covers: The Omega Nebula
Courtesy of NASA

All rights reserved. No part of this book may be reproduced in any form or by any electronic or mechanical means including information storage and retrieval systems without permission in writing from the author, except by a reviewer who may quote brief passages in a review.

Correspondence to info@delysian.com

Library of Congress Control Number:
2014919691

ISBN-13: 978-0-9836338-7-7
ISBN-10: 0-9836338-7-8

10 9 8 7 6 5 4 3 2 1

Printed in the United States of America

Harry

I love you, my Husband, my best Friend. You filled my life with joy and always made me and our children feel safe and loved.

You always reminded me: "Trust in our Heavenly Father and do not worry about tomorrow, for tomorrow will take care of itself."

I will hold on to the Love and the Life we knew, until we meet again.

I love you always and forever.

Francine

"I guess I'll go first."

—*Harry Tompkins*

*Always the first to end
the awkward silence that followed
the first question asked each week in class*

Contents

Church 1
Community 9
Doubt 15
Faith 29
Fear 39
Forgiveness 45
Free Will 53
Good & Evil 65
Grace, Justice & Law 71
Love 77
Prayer 87
Religion 111
Scripture 123
Sheep 131
Truth 135
Potpourri 151
Epitaph 157

PREFACE

THIS IS A BOOK OF THOUGHTS about spiritual topics given voice by one Harry Tompkins, of Saline, Michigan, who died without warning on 23 September, 2014 of a stroke. He was 57 years old.

Harry was a long-time member of a small group of people who attend a weekly Bible class led for 20 years by Donald W. Weaver, M.D., at the Seventh Day Adventist Church in Taylor, Michigan. Dr. Weaver has kindly written the Foreword to this book.

The class is unusual in including participants from different Christian denominations, different faiths, and sometimes people of no faith. It is unusual also in having members who participate via Skype, sometimes from as far away as India, Saudi Arabia, Canada, Hawaii, and—on one

PREFACE

memorable occasion—from Bethlehem, the birthplace of Jesus Christ.

Not least, the class is unusual in that, since August 2012, its meetings have been recorded, transcribed, and posted on a public blog called *The Interface* (www.donweaver.org). These transcripts have given his classmates an unique opportunity to memorialize Harry and share with his family, friends, and the public at large his deeper thoughts.

This is probably not a book to be read consecutively, from beginning to end. Rather, it is a book to be dipped into, at random, to savor and be surprised and elevated by spiritual insights so full of warmth and love and so revealing of the heart and soul of a man so simple, yet so profound.

David Ellis
Detroit, Michigan
October, 2014

FOREWORD

IN THE DEAD OF MORNING of the 23rd day of September in the year 2014, a once bright and steady light flickered, then went out.

For a long time afterwards, those who knew Harry Tompkins found themselves in a darker world. Gone for ever was the quick smirk, the bright eye, the easy shrug of the shoulders that told you Harry was locked into your conversation.

Harry was at the same time a complex and a simple person. Complex, because he was on a life's journey that took him down a multitude of various paths, often puzzling not only to others but confusing to himself as well; simple, because with Harry, what you saw was what you got. He wore his heart on his sleeve and bared his soul in everything he said.

FOREWORD

With Harry, life wasn't a take it or leave it proposition. For him, life was meant to be embraced with passion. Whether it was family, friends, or food, Harry always wanted to take it up a notch. Yet he had an easy way with people. He made you feel as if you were among his best friends.

He craved affection, loved to touch; and the hugs and kisses would begin whenever and wherever he showed up. But Harry's easygoing and imperturbable exterior masked a sensitive soul. His attraction to people was often mistaken for extroversion, but the truth—especially in his later years—was that he enjoyed a good book as much as a big crowd. Most of all, he cherished warm conversation with friends.

Harry was honest to the core and not given to much dissembling. He was the first to tell you he had many faults. Fortunately, what he lacked in self-discipline was readily compensated for by the ever watchful eye of his lovely Francine, who knew just how far to push—and no further. The truth is, I never saw him angry. Francine brought to Harry a degree of order, a sense of direction, and a way of keeping his feet on the ground. His resignation to her order was perhaps, at first, somewhat resented but as time went on he found

FOREWORD

it reassuring, reliable, and eventually even humorous.

For 20 years, Harry sat to my immediate left in the circle of our Bible class. It was in this context that I knew him best. Not given to much risk taking in life, Harry was a relentless risk taker of ideas. Almost always the first one to speak up in class, often to put the scripture under discussion into historical context, Harry rarely heard a new idea he didn't like.

I watched over the years as he tested and tried and refined his picture of God. It was in matters of the Spirit that his passion really showed. He said things like: "Forgiveness is like an umbilical cord to the divine; without it there is no communication with God." The last thing he said in class was this, speaking about the truth about God: "What is wrong with saying 'I simply do not know?'" This book is dedicated to the memory of Harry through the many pearls of spiritual wisdom he shared with us in class and with the world through the class blog, *The Interface*.

The sometimes contrarian nature of Harry's faith made some people uncomfortable, but his contrariness was never mean spirited and always without malice. Just the Sabbath before he died he spoke to me at length of his regret for saying anything that would disturb others.

FOREWORD

Few people gave more thought to their relationship with God than Harry. No one sent me more emails asking me questions about God and expressing thoughts concerning the Truth about God. Faith and belief do not always equal that Truth. We argue with passion that our spiritual Truth is accurate and complete for the journey of life, and then we tend to shun and ostracize those who don't share our Truth. Harry believed that what we can observe is that all humans have good within them, regardless of their religion. All know mercy, kindness, selflessness, compassion, empathy, service and trustworthiness. These attributes are the fruits of the spirit and change the world to make it a better place.

Harry saw religion in its most basic terms: Love, compassion and grace. No one felt God's grace more, no one was moved by God's grace more, no one relied on God's grace more. For Harry the spiritual journey was not an easy one, yet he never complained, and above all he never blamed God. For him there was doubt mixed with hope, pain mixed with joy, loss mixed with gain.

Harry once shared this passage with me from 1 Corinthians 15:10, quoting the apostle Paul:

> *By the grace of God, I am what I am and His grace toward me did not prove in vain, but I labored even*

FOREWORD

more than all of them, yet not I, but the grace of God with me.

Harry embraced God and God embraced Him. He was in plain truth a friend of God. Quoting again from Paul, 1 Corinthians 15:

Listen I tell you a mystery, We will not all sleep but we will all be changed, In a flash in the twinkling of an eye, at the last trumpet, for the trumpet will sound, the dead will be raised imperishable and we will be changed. For the perishable must clothe itself with the imperishable, and the mortal with immortality. When the perishable has been clothed with the imperishable, and the mortal with immortality, then the saying that is written will come true: death has been swallowed up in victory.

Where, O death is your victory? Where, O death is your sting? But thanks be to God! He gives us the victory through our Lord Jesus Christ.

Rest in peace, my dear friend.

Donald W. Weaver
Taylor, Michigan
October, 2014

CHURCH

SOMEONE HAS SAID it is the will of God that women should not be ordained as preachers. We say that Jesus saves, but saves from what? People put their own interpretations on it.

The early church was more liberal than the modern church.

There is still a large body of standard Christian doctrine behind the offbeat, divergent views of the non-mainstream views. A newcomer in a church

CHURCH

loses some of his or her individualism in order to conform, but over time, the conviction may weaken.

I often criticize the church, but it was my starting point. It's a good pre-school for spiritual life. It's good for children. There may come a point when we mature, spiritually, and our beliefs may change radically, but the church does have a contribution to make. Small communities of bygone days provided comfort and security for their members, They helped people survive. We still need that help, and we can still find it in church.

Some churches have so much doctrine and accept you only by what you believe, not by how much love you have. If you don't agree with them, you'll be ostracized or ignored. Little churches, with little in the way of structure, are truer communities.

CHURCH

In early human history, community was formed around where one was born. One was directly connected to one's immediate geophysical neighbors, but not beyond them. Today, we are born into a global community, connected by modern communication technologies. Churches tend to be pseudo communities. Real community still today can only happen in small, local, physically connected groups. True community starts with your next-door neighbor.

The principles Jesus gave us—turning the other cheek, etc.—are certainly chaos-inducing. They imply that unless we allow other people to believe what they want to believe, it's impossible to form a real community with them. For those who seek God, we provide the pseudo community of church, but true community starts with your immediate neighbors and allowing them to have their own religious and philosophical perspectives, and not try to change them and not to judge them. You must be willing to accept this chaos in order to get to peace.

CHURCH

For true inclusiveness, a community should not judge people's beliefs. If it does, it's a clique, it's judgmental. Jesus never judged Judaism—he just wanted to destroy what it did to the disenfranchised. Pseudo community is exclusive by its very nature.

Leaders can be and usually are a problem to some members of the community. I heard disturbing news about the termination of the principal at the school my kids attended, apparently because he was not conservative enough. This caused a problem for one element of the community, which did not want conservatism. Global communication may make us next door neighbors, but they don't mean our kids will attend the same school. The only way to address such issues is a community that accepts differing philosophies.

The ideal community seems unattainable, but on an individual basis it might be possible to achieve something like it. Americans who emigrate to a Catholic country, or a Buddhist country, generally

CHURCH

don't try to change the host culture and beliefs—they go along with them, and even assimilate themselves to a certain extent. All we want from community is to be cared for, to enjoy one another's company. Our problem is that we create exclusive pseudo communities.

Our class* is one of the more accepting of "other" individuals. You would think everyone would want to belong to it. Yet they don't. People want community *their* way. Others reject our philosophy—they want exclusiveness for their theology.

From discussions with my employees, it seems that the rules of religion make no sense to them. What does make sense to them is community and doing good. Church disguises goodness by ritualizing it.

---

* That is, *The Interface* discussion group. See p. *xii.*

CHURCH

The original apostles were not a part of the Pauline church. So Christianity is Pauline rather than apostolic. The first schism, or chaos, had to do with abandoning the laws of Moses. Peter had the vision in which he was told to eat from a bag full of un-kosher meat, but he couldn't get past his discomfort. In essence, the apostles were disfellowshipped, disenfranchised, from the church.

I think this class serves the purpose of keeping me alert to my inner voice, but I think others may find it disturbing and it may render them less attuned to the voice. Church used to work for me, but no longer. We must be ready to transition from one medium to another. I hear the voice through the good works of others—of Gandhi and Mother Theresa and so on.

... and Evangelism

For some believers the call to evangelize or share the good news is a responsibility that is entrusted to them from God. In their hearts they are doing

CHURCH

you a great act of kindness and offering you a life saving gift. But of course much of that perception that you must evangelize is interpretation of scripture and how the scripture is digested in the community.

Most people who are of the Christian faith and are inclined to want to share the good news or get you to believe the way they do, usually only attempt it with family members and co-workers with whom they are close.

We had a Jehovah's Witness over for dinner. She was uncomfortable talking religion. I think she was afraid I would attack her beliefs. What she wanted was friendship, not argument. So avoid it! Love people for who and what they are.

COMMUNITY

I ASKED some of my employees whether they belonged to any church or community group. One told me he did not belong to a church but belonged to a Moose Lodge, and he did so because it provided him with a sense of community and he liked the goodness of the people there. Another employee told me he belonged to a fishermen's group, but not to a church. He did so because he felt comfortable with the group and because he felt good about the occasional charitable events they organized (fish-fries, for example.)

We come to this class because we share a common faith in Goodness. Jesus is not so concerned that we believe in God, but rather that we seek the meaning of Goodness, because that is what changes lives, prevents war, removes selfishness, and tames the ego.

COMMUNITY

Why is there a wall between Israeli and Palestinian? What does it mean, and what does it matter, to have a nationality? Is there not a connection at a deeper level? Of course there is, but we set up barriers.

If you try to create a marker, or a flag, that defines community, you are stating a belief that leads automatically to pseudo community.* True community is simpler than we think. Friendship subsumes community. Out of friendship, you remain interested and concerned about what happens to your friends, and even the friends of one's friend, and community grows out of that alone. Community fails when you give it a name and say this is what this community is and believes. I am still friends with many of my childhood acquaintances, even though we have all followed divergent paths. This is a true community. It happens naturally and has no requirements.

---

* M. Scott Peck: *The Different Drum: Community Making and Peace.* Touchtone, 1998.

COMMUNITY

The average family seems not very close knit. One is closer to one's children of course, because they are part of one. Most of my closest friends from childhood are non-believers, though they are good people with attributes we would call "Christian." When we try to create community, it usually means we want to convert people to our beliefs, but true community doesn't do that.

I once thought true community was achievable only with one's near neighbors. I've changed my mind. To tell the truth, I don't want to be part of a community that is not of like mind to mine. When my neighbor's house burns down, sure, I will be very good to them for a couple of days. But if I have to put them up in my basement for six months, my attitude and behavior towards them will probably change. So I don't think this can be true community.

COMMUNITY

Jesus did not ask for wholesale changes to the community of Judaism. He just addressed points where it had failed, and he focused on the poor and sick because they are out of community. He never said Judaism was bad, or called for revolution in theology. He addressed humanity, not theology. This would be just the same if he returned today and came to our SDA church. He'd be addressing how we treat one another in time of need, etc.

... Pillars of

The more you adhere to the idea of not being a stumbling block to the development of faith in others, the further you distance yourself from community. The blessing is that you don't need community because you are closer to God. It brings a natural freedom to do such things as, for example, to visit and enjoy the true beauty of an ornate Catholic church. With the kind of freedom I am talking about, you need not judge it; instead, you can just enjoy it!

The less you say, the more other people will be exposed directly to God. They are God's responsibility, not ours.

COMMUNITY

... and The Unpardonable Sin

You commit the unpardonable sin when you disconnect yourself from humanity, when you fence yourself in (or out.) Jesus spent his ministry healing the broken hearts of people who had become disconnected in some way. The one thing we have in common is our humanity. The most disconnected I have ever been was when I shut out my fellow church members who, I thought, did not possess the light, the "Truth". That is unpardonable sin. That is blasphemy.

DOUBT

DOUBT IS PRIVATE and should only be shared in a community that has as its conviction that there is no capital-T Truth except the one that God alone can ever know. In our journeys, we progress from one lower-case-t truth to another, evolving as we journey down life's road. The only tangible immutable truth I can attest to with confidence is that we all shall die. I believe in faith that God is love and if we apply love and kindness to our neighbors we might change the world and make it a better place. Beyond that, I know nothing.'

DOUBT

Civilization evolves through uncertainty. Doubt is part of the evolutionary process of learning and growing and advancing. Either God does not exist or he does. The problem is that in trying to find a way to him we miss the simple fact of his ubiquitous presence. In a sense, maybe we can't see the real tree for the forest of trees that look real to us. Continual searching helps us to move towards the real tree, even though we may never get to hug it. Doubt protects us from the mistaken certainty that the particular tree we select (for whatever reason) is God.

To me, doubt is a positive. People can and do have different perspectives on the Bible and the writings of other religions and philosophies, but at the end of the day, if God exists, then one has to feel God tugging at one's heart. There has to be a sense of an inner God. The core principle in people of all religions and no religion is love, respect, and caring for people in need. *That*'s the proof of God's existence, not scripture. My doubts are not about God, but are about the inconsistencies of the Bible. But that's just me. We all find a path that we are comfortable with.

Does doubt encourage or discourage? Or both? Does it uplift, or push down. Does it show unity, or sow discord?

Doubt does none of those things for me. I think it depends on the individual. But for a community, it can create hesitation to participate. Doubt is not a problem for the scientific community, though: It is a virtue.

To Seventh Day Adventists who stick to the belief in six days of creation, the news in mid-2014 of a major scientific corroboration of the Big Bang theory ought to stir doubt.

The problem is that in a community of belief, belief is sacrosanct, therefore doubt is heresy.

Atheists and agnostics often spend a lot of time on the question of God. I have been through such doubt and as a result I feel closer to God than ever before. But everything has changed. What con-

DOUBT

vinces me that God exists is the evident fact that everyone is prompted by the God spark, the inner light, the holy spirit within them to search for him or at least for some deeper truths. And who knows that atheists and agnostics don't find them? Their divorce rate is lower, they are more inclined to obey the civil law, and they are quite the opposite of what a Christian might assume of them.

Doubt is not necessarily a bad thing, even it feels bad to one experiencing it. I think most doubt is about scripture itself.

If it is wrong for doubters to try to impose their doubts on believers, is it then equally wrong for believers to try to impose their beliefs on doubters?

Doubt is like a vote of no confidence in that perceived truth. When doubt takes hold in the mind it means one has just lost confidence in what one had previously held to be truth; in the very pillars of faith which, one had supposed, provided assurances of both a good life and a life after death. It affects one's participation in one's existing community of faith.

To question what you once thought was immutable can be devastating for those you love and those with whom you shared communion in your community of faith. That community by its very nature must try to rescue you from your doubt and will do so using the same tools that captivated you in the first place. It will seek to re-indoctrinate you to the principles of its perceived immutable truth, couched in love of course, and it will honestly fear that you will be lost if it can't get you back.

What do you do when you begin to doubt? Should you ignore it? Share it with others? I feel at this point in my own life and journey that doubt it is better dealt with by me alone and shared only with those I believe to have like minds. It is one thing to doubt one's own faith but quite another to create doubt in another's faith.

People who reside comfortably in a faith community are at peace with their truth. They don't want to hear that you doubt their truth and its capacity to provide security in their journey through life. Your doubt and especially your confidence in your doubt creates great anxiety in, and is seen as a threat to, the community and its individual members.

Firm faith is usually established by growth of one's community and the acceptance of such prescribed truths by others. The old adage "There's strength in numbers" emboldens them to think they must be right, since so many others think the same way as they do.

I personally do not see that sharing one's doubts in a community set in its faith is a good thing. It might even be evil. I came to my own doubts by a thought process that was within me. To share my doubt with others who are not asking the same questions would be wrong and selfish. By doing so I would be trying to get them to confirm my own conclusions so I might be even more at peace with my choices.

... and Jacob

It is hugely significant that God does not seek to blame, accuse, or correct Jacob in any way. This God does not fit the standard picture of him, and is hardly the God of Israel.

... and Elijah

It sounds to me like Elijah had self doubt. He misjudged God, he misjudged the support for God. The lesson is that we are clueless about God.

DOUBT

... Origin of

At face value (that is, the value of the words of Genesis alone, shorn of the spin we have learnt or been taught to put on them) the Garden of Eden was replete with doubt. To be "crafty" and to challenge the word of God as it did, the serpent must have had less than complete faith in God. It then contaminated Adam and Eve with the same doubts about, and challenge to, the authority and power of God's word.

But (and again, these are essentially the words of scripture, not an inference) they were not thrown out of heaven because of their doubts about God: They were thrown out because, once their eyes were opened to good and evil, God did not want them to eat of the Tree of Life and become immortal. Those are what the words of the scripture tell us, plainly and simply. Now, we may infer that perhaps God knew they would do evil once they knew about evil, but but it is hardly an inference to say that there certainly was doubt in the Garden of Eden before the Fall.

And, by the way, the doubt seems to have been destructive doubt insofar as it destroyed at least some of Adam and Eve's faith.

... and Innocence

Children question everything yet, for the most part, are troubled by nothing. To them, the world is not a fearsome place and Truth is not all that important. I think that God cares less that we understand who he is than that we regain a childlike sense of serenity.

... Positive and Negative

Despite a long history, in both scriptural and historical record, of faith in God seemingly having no power to ward off disaster, faith remains. It's not that things get any clearer; it's just that it still feels right to have faith. God doesn't really answer Job's question, but Job goes on to live a long, happy life.

... and Theodicy

Theodicy is about the question: Why does God allow evil? The answer is: It is just a fact of life.

DOUBT

Belief in God does not exempt one from it. God's concern in Genesis 3:22...

> *Then the Lord God said, "Behold, the man has become like one of Us, knowing good and evil; and now, he might stretch out his hand, and take also from the tree of life, and eat, and live forever."*

... is because (as was revealed earlier in the book) Adam and Eve's understanding of their new knowledge of good and evil was skewed. They were like God in *knowing* good and evil, but not in *understanding* that knowledge. That seems to me to be the only reason why God would not want them to be immortal and instead drove them out of heaven and padlocked the gate.

Our view of what is good and what is bad is not the same as God's view, and the proof of that can be seen in the fact that evil has always persisted on the Earth over which God gave us dominion, whereas it was not present in Eden, where God has dominion.

... and Religion

Doubt is extremely problematic to a faith-based community. When reaching out or defending their community, its members point to the immutability of their truth as a reason why you should join or believe as they do. When people agree with them and join, it strengthens the group's faith in its perceived truth.

... and Fear and Death

Most Christians are motivated by the belief that their particular "faith" will bring them security in this life and in the next. To deviate from this belief is to face death, which invokes fear. So their "faith" gives them a sense of superiority through the belief that their lives are built on the one-and-only rock of truth.

That's why I read scripture for what it actually says rather than for what I would like it to say. It can lead one down some very dark paths, but that seems to be where God wants us to go. God's message is: "I created you. I love you. Go and find your way. You can be sure of my grace. I will protect you, but in ways you cannot fathom."

... and Fear and Stages of Faith

Fear, doubt, and disillusionment are necessary parts of the transition process. Faith stage 5, which is simply faith in and practice of universal love, helps one through any transition.[†] It helps one, for example, recognize the spiritually valuable and valid lessons in the Bible even after one has ceased to believe that the Bible itself is the word of God. It follows that it helps one find similar value and validity and truth in the texts of other religions. A person in stage 5 seeks God's word wherever it may be. A God who spoke only through, say, the Christian Bible would be a pretty small God!

[†] M. Scott Peck, in *The Different Drum* (see footnote p. 10) described four stages of faith. Harry and his classmates invented a fifth.

... and Inner Light and Stages of Faith

The inner light helps one get past disillusionment and through the transition to a higher stage of faith. Disillusionment is part of the process.

... Healthy

Doubt is healthy and it should be encouraged. "Truth" that once seemed immutable does in fact mutate, but that does not have to affect one's faith, or one's faith community, provided that one's faith and one's community are not based on the shifting sand of presumed-immutable mutable "truth." Church tends to deny that truth is mutable. I suspect that most individual churchgoers do not really share their church's certainty. God is much more flexible about doubt in him than his church is, as you can see in the stories of Jacob, Thomas, and so on.

FAITH

WHEN TALKING ABOUT FAITH, we need to be sure of what we are talking about: Faith *in what*? In what I believe? In my religion? In my church? In God? To me, God's existence and his love are the broad, all-encompassing objects of faith. The hermeneutics of any given "faith," belief system, or religion limit one to its interpretations of God's word.

The past 30 days have been extremely stressful at work. Our employees are by and large street people. If I have to let them go, I know I am sending them back to the street or to "the system." I am taking away so much from them, and I feel their pain. As we took up our discussion of community in this class, I again asked myself: "What do I believe in?"

FAITH

And the answer was: "I have many beliefs, which can and do change, but I have a singular and unchanging faith in Goodness." I believe that faith is shared by everyone, no matter their religion or lack thereof.

Blind faith says to me: "There is no road to follow, because I am there. There is no pathway to me, because I am everywhere. Just know that I am with you, everywhere and all the time." This gives one the freedom to live one's life to the fullest, without need for a specified path.

What is the faith Paul wants us to have? Is it faith in Jesus? Faith in his acts? Paul is none too specific. What is the spirit? Is it the part of me that leads me to good thoughts? If nothing can separate us from God's love, what is his love doing for me right now? What does it mean?

FAITH

In historical context, Paul claimed to be a "Jew of Jews." He had been taught by some of the greatest religious scholars of his day, who believed in strict adherence to the law—to rules whose observance proved one's worthiness before God. But in the gospels, he says to forget these rules, to live by faith alone. No wonder, then, that he concluded we no longer know how to pray, when we have thrown away the law, the rule book. I think Paul's own insecurity and indecisiveness is evident here. He doesn't know what to do.

I used to think that faith meant believing in Jesus. Now, I too am uncertain about what it means.

The big point Paul made was that God is there for us no matter what. I have—but I don't know about you—an inner sense, a conviction, that God exists; therefore, that he should care for me is indeed comforting and calming. My conviction that God exists cannot be explained in any way other than as an article of faith. I see the spirit of God within me whenever I feel compassion for abused animals or wish the violence in the world would all end. I think it is that simple.

Faith can be present in anyone and everyone, scientist and religionist alike. Faith does not prevent them from enjoying and practicing the culture and rituals of religion or the culture and methods of science, because religious ritual and scientific method are made by and for themselves, not for God.

I believe in God because I see goodness everywhere. Religion and church and scripture are in some ways a result of that innate goodness, and indeed they have served to maintain my awareness of goodness and have kept me in tune with the inner voice. But they are not the only way. Good atheists must have other ways to maintain their awareness, even though they deny the very concept of an inner voice or light.

... and Ego

Ego seems to be the issue with Faith. Ego is the "unreal" or "false" person we develop into as a result of the knowledge we acquire and the teaching we receive. When one is born, one has no ego, and one is truly one's self, the real you. I take issue with the concept of Belief, but I agree with the concept of Faith, in the certainty that something just is, something is truly original. We know that the sun exists. We know that gravity exists. We don't "believe" they exist–we know it to our core. So it is with God. He just is. There is nothing to fear. With faith, one becomes a part of God and brother or sister to everyone. You know that what you see in your brothers and sisters is not really them. Rebirth for me now means the death of ego. Belief stems from a fear of not knowing.

... and the Stages of Faith

Stage 1 people don't value religion. They just want to get on with their lives, and have no time for religion or spiritual things.

A stage 4 person probably has no problem with evolution or science in general, so any discussion between that person and a stage 2 person (who probably does take issue with the theory of evolution) is bound to provoke discord. The latter believes that the Bible is the literal word of God and therefore the biblical story of creation must be true. The former attacks that fundamental belief by saying that there may be much truth in the Bible but it is not the word of God.

The model is missing a stage 5: A stage of love and acceptance of all. A stage 5 person would not have that discussion at all. There is no need to interfere in the beliefs of others. A philosophy of love and acceptance views all stages of faith as valid.

Which stage we end up in is more a matter of personality. Different personalities are drawn to different stages.

Stage 2 people generally cannot deal with stage 3 people. When challenged, stage 2 people will rally in defense of their community.

I have transitioned, but I'm not sure why, and I had no control over the process. I recall I was somewhat afraid during the transition. When one is firmly ensconced in stage 2, and believes therefore that one possesses The Real and Tangible Truth, then even to think about moving away from it, to question it, understandably creates enormous tension and anxiety. Yet one can get past those anxieties, as I did, and move forward.

I think persons transitioning from 2 to 3 should leave church, otherwise they risk harming others who are secure in their stage 2 faith, or at least of causing great discomfort on both sides. The possibility for honest and free dialog would be constrained, even if mutual love were not lost. Stage 2 people might even mistake another's advance to stage 3 as a regression to stage 1. Stage 2 is a necessary foundation for stage 3.

So it seems to me, since people will tend to return to church when they reach stage 4, that church does not need to try to hold on to people, to keep them in stage 2 at all costs.

FAITH

I have been through faith stages 2 and 3, and sometimes 4 and even 1, then went back to 2 for the sake of my children who, I thought, would benefit from being brought up in my Seventh Day Adventist church community. It was the safe choice. But I can't help questioning things; not so much in search of "the Truth" as to find out why some things make no sense. Questioning is what has driven me back through the stages to where I am now. It is a natural process.

People in faith stage 2 would not accept the premise that judgment and salvation are independent of one's stage of faith, but it seems true to me. Perhaps one reason people do not progress from stage to stage is because God already exists in their hearts, and that is all that is needed for faith.

When I was in faith stage 2 I prayed and it felt good. Now I have transitioned, prayer does nothing for me. The acquisition of knowledge can help one transition if one is not frightened of the

FAITH

knowledge, if one feels liberated by it; or it can deter one from transitioning if one is frightened of the knowledge.

Faith stage 1 is clearly a bad place to be. In it, one is shiftless and self-centered. In stage 2, one has some structure and belief to hold onto. In stage 3 one comes to view God as a universal God present in all religions and all people. In stage 4, one uses stage 2 to continue to seek, and to bestow, enlightenment. There may be a stage 5, in which one simply loves and accepts everybody.

FEAR

WHEN YOU KNOW that you are eternal, death does not matter to you. Because God is inside us, there are times when our ego disappears and we risk our lives for others. We don't fear death and we should not, since we are eternal. We can still be hunter gatherers yet be cautious and risk averse.

Fear is the enemy. When you learn to deal with fear through faith, you win. Fear is the great paralyzer of mankind. It is Satan's best weapon.

FEAR

If you can come out of the desert without fear, you can live happily in the garden, in the destination, in harmony with others.

People are generally fearful. If one can overcome the fear of death, of poverty, of failure, then one is invincible. As long as one is fearful, one cannot be said to be successful. People like Mother Theresa and the Dalai Lama were/are undaunted at the prospect of failure. Prayer will not prevent a hurricane, but fearlessness can help one handle it.

... and Faith

I came close to death on a small boat during a storm on Lake Erie. Our anchor line got tangled with a buoy line as the wind and waves rose and the lightning flashed around us. I was sure I was about to die and I started to pray, but suddenly a wave lifted us up and our anchor freed itself from the buoy line. I was still afraid—of the lightning, and so on. Though I didn't die, I remained filled with the fear of death. For years afterwards I would not go back out fishing. In their storm, the disciples were just as afraid. Most of our fears are really unfounded. It is our fear of fear that inhibits faith.

... and Community

We are all filled with fear of death, etc. The "fringe" churches show a strong sense of conviction, and that helps foster a sense of security.

...and Death

When one becomes religious, or tries to become spiritual, perhaps one is looking for insulation from pain, a guarantee that things will be better, that tragedy will be avoided. But I saw a TV documentary in which a crocodile grabbed a wildebeest, whose eyes were filled with terror. That's Nature, red in tooth and claw. The bad news of a child's death delivered to its mother on Christmas Eve? That is nature too.

People go to church hoping thereby to prevent these things happening, hoping to stop nature in its tracks. But it just doesn't work that way. To deny that chaos can touch you is futile. The gift that God gives you is not to protect you from nature, it is to tell you that you are not alone.

...and Innocence

I have heard my name called from out of nowhere, when I was a child, but each time it scared me.

...and War and Peace

Jesus is a man of peace, yet he is accompanied by a disciple armed with a sword.

...and Will

Given the enormity of the blessing he was about to both receive from God and to bestow upon mankind, one would think Jesus would have run joyously to the cross. But he was troubled and heartbroken. He was like us. He was displaying his human weakness in his feelings, but also he showed his divine strength in subordinating those feelings to the will of God.

FORGIVENESS

THE RELATIONSHIP between illness and sin is clear. A book by a physician describes cases where guilt-laden patients did indeed get better after being forgiven. But in providing a litany of bad things that will result if one does not emulate God's perfection, Leviticus also unwittingly reveals that the guilt such passages impose on believers may be the cause of their illnesses.

Yes, this is radical. Jesus lays waste to Old Testament concepts. When we forgive others, God forgives us. We have to forgive others for their ignorance. Somehow, organized religion lost its way with regard to this point in its earliest days, perhaps for reasons of power and control.

What is God's purpose in wanting to forgive us? We think it allows us to go to a higher plane when we die, but that seems to me a shallow view of forgiveness. It seems to me there must be a functional purpose that has to do with God's creation.

... and Community

To live in a community, one must accept others in the community as being like oneself. To my dismay, I find myself to be a prejudiced person. Many of my staff at work are from the lowest social strata. They are the working poor, uneducated, angry, and culturally off my measurement scale.

But to treat them with love and respect—to accept them for who they are, which is in a sense "forgiving" them—I must identify with them; I must regard and treat them as my equals. I must be able to sit down with them, eat with them, understand where they came from, be interested in their lives and their culture, and offer them help when I can.

It would be much easier if I could just ignore them—if I could just manage them, give them their paycheck, and wash my hands. But this would not create community within the plant. To me, the question is: Is forgiving others going to do something for God in this world? I think it does. I think it creates community.

... for God's Sake

Forgiveness is like an umbilical cord to the divine. Without it, there can be no communion with God. In the Old Testament, God seems very interested in telling us how he wants to forgive and forget our sins; whereas in the gospels, Jesus seems to emphasize the necessity of our forgiveness of others even more, to the point of denying us entry to the kingdom of heaven unless we do so. And forgiveness applies not only between individuals, but also between classes of individuals.

... a Trap

It's almost as though Jesus is setting a trap for us. He is teaching the principle of forgiveness. So you are inevitably going to end up having to forgive people all the time because the need for it is never ending. If you follow Jesus' teaching, you will tend to be of a forgiving nature, but if you follow religious rules and ritual, you will not. The trap is where Jesus says, in effect: "When all human efforts at conflict resolution have failed, then treat the recalcitrant renegade as you would a gentile or as a tax collector." His contemporary audience would have taken that to mean "treat them with contempt," except for those who heard his thoughts about gentiles and tax collectors, who would have taken him to mean "treat them as people most in need, and most deserving, of forgiveness."

... and Conflict Resolution

I deal at work with a largely uneducated workforce lacking the education and the intellect to discuss conflicts in an informed and rational manner. To be disrespected through something as innocuous as a baleful glance can easily result in conflict. My approach is to ask the aggrieved party, in private, to explain exactly what happened.

Frequently, that exercise, while stressful to me, usually suffices to show the person that the issue was not really such a big deal, and it often reduces or eliminates the conflict.

... and Family

The Prodigal parable takes place within a family, whereas the Unmerciful Servant parable[‡] takes place among neighbors, not family. The latter is about forgiveness of one neighbors, about loving one's neighbor as oneself.

... Liberating

Forgiveness is a liberating way of life. It's hard to swallow one's ego and accept insults and forgive those who trespass against us, but the more one practices this way of life, the less conflict.

[‡] Matthew 18:21-35

... On the Cross

On the very cross, Jesus forgave and reconciled with those who killed him, and his crucifixion bestowed life on the world. His ministry in life, too, was essentially all about forgiveness and reconciliation. It was not about the form of religion, but about loving one's neighbor.

... and the Prodigal Son

The prodigal son never seems to think about his father, only about his own distress. He seeks only to assuage his own hunger.

We want the elder son to be punished, but the father did not.

In the Parable of the Prodigal Son, the elder son was in a sense tortured at the end. Even though he was treated kindly by his father, he apparently remained unhappy—tortured, as it were—about the whole thing.

I would never allow my son to make bad choices if I had control. That is because I am driven by my fear of what might happen to my son. But in this case, God is the father, and God is in control.

... and Reconciliation

Reconciliation can be a one-way street—you can reconcile with someone even if they don't respond. To put this in perspective, in the beginning, there was just one "tree" with two branches, or perhaps I should say a trunk and one branch: God and wo/man. There were no Jews then. They were grafted onto this tree later. As was everyone else. We have no ability to graft ourselves onto this tree—to reconcile ourselves with God; only he can graft us in. But what is typically taught is that we can reconcile ourselves with him through penance and other behavioral mechanisms and modification.

... Universal

God forgives everybody, but the trait does not come easily to us. Maybe Jesus did say the bit about torture in the Parable of the Unmerciful Servant, just to drive home the point.

FREE WILL

BEING FORCED to sit at home following surgery has given me time to contemplate many things, and one of the things I enjoy contemplating is what we talk about in class. I wanted to share some of my thoughts with you. Your input would be appreciated. These are just thoughts. I have no idea if I am on to something or not but these ideas do intrigue me.

I have been thinking about God's will versus our free will, and about prayer, and about by what authority does free will exist.

It hit me like a ton of bricks! The authority comes from us. We give ourselves the authority to call something Holy or sacred. It may be a prayer, a book, a place… any thing. The choice is ours to make something Holy or sacred. In light of our class discussion of free will verse God's will, it dawned on me that none of these so called Holy things has the authority to pronounce whether something is God's will because its authority—its holiness, its sacredness—was determined by us. Holy things exist only because we authorized their existence. In short: They are holy because we say they are, not because of some unmistakable intrinsic quality.

For example: The Bible is the word of God because someone chose to believe and say it was. But the only way any of us can be sure that something came from God is if God hands it to us directly or we personally witness its delivery by God to someone else. Absent that personal witness, the validity of any argument about what is truth, based upon these holy things, is suspect at best. It is not necessarily wrong to argue points of truth based on human determination of what is holy; we have done it through the ages and it has blessed people's lives. But where does that leave us in our quest for God's will in our life, for the kingdom of heaven? What can we take out of the Bible or any holy book that men arbitrarily claim to be God's will?

I believe that we as individuals are the only real determinant of holy authenticity; not by creating it, but by acknowledging our conscience—our inner sense of what is right or wrong or merciful.

FREE WILL

It is built into us. All people have a conscience, regardless of their creed or religion. I do not believe that people have had to learn about conscience in some sort of historical or evolutionary process: I believe it just exists within us, and always has. We know from history that many people through the ages exhibited a conscience. I believe Jesus exhibited it. from the accounts of his life.

Those accounts may have been somewhat skewed through the error and embellishment that accompanies verbal storytelling, but there is enough of it from several sources to satisfy many of us that the direction in which he was going is clear.

My point is that Jesus had the same traits of justice, mercy, and love instilled in him by the same creator as us. He taught us about these traits in a world that he called the kingdom of heaven, but I think a better translation would be the kingdom of Conscience. We all possess this this conscience, these traits, this knowledge. It is original—unique—and in the first person because it is us. We need to take our cue from Jesus and implement the kingdom of Conscience in society. It is not what we say or preach; it is what we do. We need to relearn this. We have been taught to look outside ourselves, to others' definitions of these traits, and have been told that we must earn them. But conscience is in all of us and is recognizable to others when it is applied as from God. Mother Theresa is an example of a woman who lived her conscience. All religions recognize her as a woman who did God's will. Probably the best proof of her doing God's will was her own doubt about the faith she was brought up in, because it probably didn't totally harmonize with her conscience.

... vs. God's Will

Jesus subjugated his will to God's and lost his life as a result. He didn't fight in any way. What effect did this have on those who followed him, as well as on those who crucified him? Not what you'd expect! Yet Judaism lost out in a very real way, while Christianity gained greatly.

I go back and forth. I am naturally rebellious, though in certain circumstances I may find peace in conformity. On the one hand we have free will, and end up with global warming, or personal suc-

FREE WILL

cess; but it's also destructive—you achieve it by hurting others. What strikes me about the Lord's Prayer is that everybody and every church tries to define what God's will is. To me, it's a statement of fact: God's kingdom will come, his will will be done. Your will doesn't matter; at the end of the day, it's his will, not yours, that will be done.

Our will has no bearing on God's will. We have exercised our free will, at least since the Fall, on our own perception of what is right and good; on our own perception of the law. God's perception of right and good and the law is different. The wedding guests were rounded up regardless of whether they were good or bad, rich or poor.

Their free will didn't matter to God. Regardless of what they chose, in the end, it was God's will that was done. If you choose the principles of forgiveness, love, etc., then you are already in the kingdom. The prodigal's elder brother was in the kingdom but was miserable. He was not willing to wear the garment of nakedness, the garment of the wedding feast.

Theology tries to define God's will, and ostracizes those who don't approve the theologian's interpretation. Jesus is trying to say that the kingdom comes and God's will will be done regardless. If Christianity creates peace, helps people survive, then it seems to have no negatives. In our deepest pride, we want to say that we know the truth and you have to see it my way. This is what leads to trouble—we judge, we don't forgive. Jesus says not to judge one another because no-one knows the real Truth.

... and the Old Testament

The Old Testament was written for the Children of Israel, who had free will up to a point. Nobody else did. Pharaoh had no choices—he was manipulated by God. Psalm 136 is Israel's celebration of God's intervention with Pharaoh. Free will started to evolve in the latter part of Israel's existence.

... and the Ego

We think we know God, but we don't. Paul says you are going to live and die in God, so just let go of your ego. Leave it alone, and it will come to its own conclusions.

... and Love and Fear

Fear is created when we preconceive how things should be done. We insulate ourselves within that preconception. Church communities want their members to think like one another, and even to do business only with other members of the church.

Some scriptural authors talk of an evolution toward true community, and say that true community is inclusive, not exclusive. So the message is that the "others" who are not of this fold are also not of the same mind and not of the same beliefs, yet they must be allowed in. That is very troublesome to many people, who mistake the scriptural

FREE WILL

message to mean that in entering our fold, the "other" will be transformed to become like us. That is not the case, and that invokes fear.

To love somebody who does not think and believe like oneself is the bridge that God asks us to cross in order to reach true community. The ability to love, and the recognition that God is in control, unshackles us from our attachment to our own beliefs, and therefore to our fears. Christians believe that chaos comes from evil, but the evidence suggests that God gives us chaos in order to help us escape our fears.

Companies can be hit by financial setbacks requiring hard business decisions. So managers make cuts and move forward, but the impacts they have on people's lives are horrific. Many employees cannot "bounce back" if laid off. If I am their manager, I am the end of their line.

When you realize what you have to do in the name of something or other (in this case, business) to other people, you see how far we are from following the teachings of Jesus.

We need to be able at an individual level to touch and spread goodness. We have to be able to get out of ourselves. I try to find another job for the employees I lay off. But many business managers are too distant, they don't see the suffering, the torment, the fear in the faces of people they cause to be laid off. Community sets rules that skew the meaning of goodness, and make it harder.

Knowledge is power. I couldn't speak with authority about Lego building blocks, but Jay[§] could, because he knows everything there is to know about Lego. But we should be prepared to speak our minds anyway, however imperfectly. If we hold back out of fear, we are in pseudo, not true, community.

[§] Jay is a member of the class from which this book was derived.

FREE WILL

Everybody is different. I myself find myself kicking against the pseudo community known as church. But love is real. It leads you to accept people whether or not they think like you, whether or not they frustrate you. So my chosen path is to get to know, and love, my next door neighbor as compared to my more distant fellow churchgoer.

Everyone has a different path to the kingdom of heaven. Pseudo community may be a necessary beginning—it can get us started on a path, help us create friendships. But the true path is not dictated by the pseudo community—it must be self-generated.

The kingdom of heaven is about what your heart tells you to do, and not to judge others who take different paths. In this sense, being an individual but accepting all other individuals is where the kingdom of heaven is. It allows you to integrate with everybody. But once you limit yourself with a creed, you ostracize people. If you were to walk into a church and ask to join the kingdom of heaven, you would first be expected to learn their ways, their liturgy, etc., first, rather than just saying "Yes, you are a brother (or sister) according to the Bible".

We must realize that neither we nor the "other" possesses The Truth. Only God knows The Truth. We may possess truth with a small t, but it is subject to change. To be able to grow, to find true community, we must love people because ultimately they are on the same journey we ourselves are on, no matter how different we may be in all other respects.

Most families are dysfunctional except with regard to one thing: Their children. With few exceptions, we never stop loving our children, we never stop accepting them, regardless of conflict with them. Mothers of mass murderers still visit their sons in prison. In pseudo communities, that kind of love and acceptance does not exist.

FREE WILL

Most people are afraid of missing the goal for which their community was established (for example, the goal of a church community is to get to heaven) if the goal, or the belief underlying it, changes. Or, they are afraid of admitting they were wrong to believe in the community goals and precepts to begin with.

We can't prove our beliefs are correct, versus (say) those of the (more numerous) Buddhists.

We are more arrogant among our own people, our own community.

GOOD & EVIL

ADAM AND EVE developed a flawed idea of good and evil as a result of eating the fruit. Evil exists; it needs to exist; it just is.

The question "Who is the greatest in the kingdom of heaven?" was a very selfish question. It had nothing to do with Goodness, which is the whole point of the kingdom. Goodness is what connects us to God; it's where I place my faith.

I was trying to explain this to a non-religious person at work who took me to mean I did not believe in God. I said I had faith in God because

God was Goodness, but as for belief, there are too many versions of God to believe in! There's the Bible version, the Koran version, the Buddhist version, and so on. But they share the common thread of Goodness, and Goodness is what we all seek. Jesus taught Goodness, not religion! He taught how to find Goodness in community so we could bring the kingdom of God into being. Goodness is God.

... and Our Image of God

The shooting of small children at Sandy Hook Elementary in December 2012 was evil. A person who can be so angry or sick is a psychopath and a psychopath does not share our sense of right and wrong. As a young man, I hurt people. It's a terrible feeling and it stays with you. It's an adrenalin-filled event at the time, but when it's over you feel horrible.

To continue hurting people after the adrenaline subsides is evil. If this guy was a psychopath, the act was not evil for him. Some people would consider some aspects of my lifestyle to be evil. It depends on how we define evil. The problem is when we try to say how God defines it. Why did

God not want Adam and Eve to live in heaven for eternity with the knowledge of Good and Evil? Maybe it's because we don't know what Good and Evil mean to God. Maybe this act was not evil in God's mind.

The 2nd Commandment warns us off "graven images." Constructing an image of God means more than building an idol, it means constructing him from everything we know, it means constructing him to fit our personality, our values.

The problem for Adam and Eve was not in eating the apple, it was (Genesis 3:22):

> *Then the Lord God said, "Behold, the man has become like one of Us, knowing good and evil; and now, he might stretch out his hand, and take also from the tree of life, and eat, and live forever…"*

The problem philosophically was that Adam and Eve now had the knowledge of good and evil. Since they were already like Gods—living in heaven and with eternal life—why was this a problem?

We place value on good and evil, and imbue our images of God with them. When something happens that does not fit the image of God we have created, we grow perplexed and even angry.

The problem is we don't know how to define evil. We've created an image—a paradigm—of a God who is like us; yet he is not like us. We want him to have the same sympathies and feelings as us, and to come to our defense when our sensibilities are offended. But look at the evidence that he does not, in fact, do so: In just recent history, Hitler and Pol Pot killed six and seven million people respectively! There was evil and destruction on a massive scale, yet God did not intervene. We want him to, but throughout history, he has never intervened.

It does not mean he does not exist. But our perception of who God is and how he functions is our problem. The last six of the Ten Commandments are pretty simple: love your mother and father, don't steal, commit adultery, murder, etc. These are things that create anger and pain etc. Obeying the commandments results in a peaceful life. But you are still going to die.

Mike Huckabee's magic pill of a God in the classroom to protect children is a myth. The evidence is flat against it. God wants us to survive and to do good to others, but evil is with us: We sell guns to people, we do things that create pain. God has nothing to do with that. God is about telling us how to live. This is not to say there is not something magical about God.

God is within us, and there are magical moments when we are on the same plane with him. But the image of God we have created through theology is poisonous.

... Goodness

Goodness is found within persons of all beliefs and no beliefs. Goodness uses the spirit to touch all of us. The only thing that matters is that you listen to it. When you do listen, you find yourself spreading it around—extending mercy and grace to fellow humans. You find men and women working to cure illness. You find people giving of their time and money to educate the young.

... and Salvation

Some people have no idea about God, yet will be saved because they have goodness. They might not know God as he is taught in the Bible, but if God exists at all, he exists in the heart, and that means in everyone's heart. So where there is Goodness, there is God.

GRACE, JUSTICE & LAW

IT IS GOD'S GRACE TO GIVE, not ours to beg.

The Prodigal Son's self-realization was immaterial. It's all down to the father, who could not have cared less whether his son was contrite or not. He just wanted his son back. The message is that it doesn't matter what you want. You will get grace, no matter what you do, no matter what is done to you.

GRACE, JUSTICE & LAW

Given that grace is a free pass to do whatever we want, the immediate question becomes: What, then, do we want? I think the answer is: We want peace.

The Justice talked about in Isaiah is not really the kind of justice Man wants. We have created our own selfish doctrine of justice but it cannot compare with that of a God whose ways are not our ways, whose thoughts are not our thoughts. We (myself included) are not prepared give anything like what we are supposed to give to relieve suffering and oppression. It's really quite depressing.

Billions of people born through the ages have never read "the law" and never heard of the Bible, yet they live or lived the law in their hearts. Jesus ridiculed the Pharisees for their insistence on the law. And look at how the law confused Paul! He finally figured out that Jesus has us covered, and we don't need to worry about it.

Yes, the law is from man and is flawed. That's why Jesus was mocking it. It's so flawed that it is impossible to uphold.

If you believe that God exists, the only true law is inside you, even though you may not understand it. We are naturally spiritual. The Pharisees based the law on their understanding of good and evil, but remember that God said "My ways are not your ways"—there's no way you can understand my concepts. So our understanding of good and evil may not be God's—they are man-made. So Joyce is right—we should not judge ourselves based on these laws. They are fundamentally corrupt. Even our concept of God is corrupt.

The question is: Where does the law reside? In our hearts, or in some man-made, and manifestly imperfect, construct?
Jesus told us to "turn the other cheek." This and other laws that God wrote were written in human hearts long before the Ten Commandments appeared. Every human who has ever been born has the law in his or her heart. The problem is setting up laws and saying that they are the way to God.

We cannot have faith and love as strong as God's. That's life. One has days when one fails, and days when one succeeds, in following rules. We should listen to God in our heart, and try to love our neighbor as ourselves even though we know we will often fail. In Jesus we have the perfect example of including everyone—*everyone*—in community and telling us plainly that laws and biblical exhortations that *exclude* are false.

The tares in the parable of the Wheat and the Tares are the Mosaic law and the prophets. We are known by our actions, not by our beliefs.

The problem is that what we do in our community has nothing to do with our relationship with God.

Law vs. Grace

Most people don't want grace. They prefer the law. Maybe the law came after the Fall. Maybe it's our attempt to put ourselves back into God's good graces by showing him that we abide by the law.

If we choose to live by the law, grace is an objectionable thing. We might not say so openly, but we hate it when someone gets something for nothing. After all, we've worked hard for what we've got. We can measure it in many ways. We deserve a just reward! Or so we think. But the fact is, you can't do this intellectually, empirically, or through measurement, at all. You can only choose, or not, the way that our great teachers—Jesus, Buddha, etc.—taught will change our lives and those of others and bring us the greatest joy.

... and Oxygen

We can see neither oxygen nor grace, we do not perceive them, we are not consciously aware of them. Yet we make an issue of grace. It reminds me of the passages where God says words to the effect "You don't know me, I'm not where you think I am." The mystery of grace is that it just is. There is no way of finding it or manufacturing it. We should just be at peace with that. I think God just wants us to accept it.

... and Life and Death

Indeed, grace does not bestow earthly life upon us. If our plane is going to crash, we are going to die like the animals we all are.

LOVE

I WOULD LIKE to get into a place where I don't care about some things. I have suffered tragic loss, and cared deeply about it; but in the end, life goes on anyway, so was the caring necessary?

The more I look at love and hurt the more I understand that they encompass a huge spectrum of emotions and human insecurities that apply to me as well.

Yet it seems that some people are born with a sense of compassion and selfless love. I don't know if it is how they were raised or genetic. Or maybe it is just my assumption that they were this way their whole life; but nevertheless they exhibit comfort with people from all four levels. Most of these individuals that I know are in level 4.

My beliefs, like those of the majority of us uneducated folks, were formulated by a family-influenced sense of duty to adhere to a faith system out of familial love and obligation. Many of us in this category are dysfunctional or come from a dysfunctional background, which would reflect the reasons we are in one or other of the "stages of faith" described by M. Scott Peck.** We who are uneducated do not apply scientific principles of measurement to our faith or our relationship to others.

It seems to me that if we did measure our faith system and our relationship to humanity, we would move to a higher level. But that takes a willingness to be educated and a self-assuredness that everything will be OK when we do search for the truth.

The problem with a good many of us is that we do not really care about the truth. We are too fearful to move forward because we base our beliefs in Magic and the so called "safety in numbers." It is said that where there is true love, there is no room for fear. Love is fearless and freeing.

** In *The Different Drum*. See footnote on p. 10.

First you have to love yourself. You can do that when you know and accept that God is with you. If you are afraid, it is because you are keeping God out. Love yourself, then you can start to love others.

I love people and animals in a way that I cannot say I love God. I cannot find an emotional connection with God. But I can see that he loves me, and I can reciprocate by trying to emulate that love in my behavior to others. I can say I love mankind with all my heart, but I cannot say I love God with all my heart.

... of God

How does one love God? What's the definition of loving God? In my opinion, God is not looking for adoration; he is looking for our action.

LOVE

... and Ministry

New York Times op-ed columnist Maureen Dowd may or may not herself be spiritual, but in getting a Catholic priest to write one of her columns[††] she was definitely meeting the needs of people in search of spirituality. It was a timely article, too, given that there is so much tragedy taking place. Close to home: The son of one of my employees died in a car crash on Christmas eve. The police came to tell the poor woman.

To me, the article shone like a beacon. It caused a paradigm shift in my thinking about Jesus. What really resonated with me was that the priest who wrote it really did not *want* to visit with a grieving family that had just lost a child. But it was his duty as a priest to do so.

All he did was sit with the family, not knowing what to say, so saying little. He was just there for them. Jesus helps people in a similar way. When we help people who are hurting, we too, in a very real sense, become God. Jesus told the Jewish priests: "If you have seen me, then you have seen the Father." He is saying that "You have to be my representative to people in their time of need, in

---

[††] 'Why, God?' *New York Times*, December 25, 2012.

times of chaos." Jesus wants us to intervene *for him* in chaos. That is the cross we must bear.

Our emphasis on personal piety and religion, which says self-justification is a form of Godliness, robs God of who he wants us to be, and how he wants us to be. It's not your theology that matters—it's your love; it's the time you spend with people in need. God wants us to know very little about him, except that he is Love. Everything else dies, but Love persists. It is life-changing, not only for the ministered-to but also for the minister.

The toolbox of the priest who wrote the Dowd column [see previous homily] did not seem to include "comforters," tools for consoling. When visiting a grieving family that had lost a child, he just sat at the hospital with them, not saying much, for the most part. But by his presence he was letting them know they were not alone. He was just being there.

In situations like that, we think we have to act; we think we must do something. But that's not so. Just by being there, we experience their chaos, we live their crisis. Everybody can do that. You can't stop someone from grieving over a lost child, but what you can do is say "I am with you. You are not alone in your grief."

... and Ego and Community

It's almost impossible to love one's neighbor if one has ego. The Boston bombing[‡‡] is a crystal clear case of an ego-driven act. If you strip away the ego from the bomber, then you can have sympathy for him–for the real him, not the false him who did the bombing. How do you get to the kingdom of heaven which Jesus (in Matthew) says is at hand? You don't just find a place, a community, a belief, to join. You abandon your ego, you empty yourself and allow God to drive you. Then you are in the kingdom.

[‡‡] The attack at the Boston Marathon in 2013.

... and Fay

What impressed me the most about Faten's journey* was her conviction that she was sometimes in total union with God. I think we all feel that sometimes, but Faten was lucky enough to recognize it.

... and Selfishness

We all want to do good, to help others—at least we who are "normal," not brain damaged. God comes to all people, and all people do good things. It makes God happy. And yet in the midst of bombings and other atrocities that are destroying lives still, selfish humanity is using them to score political points over gun control, etc.

---

* See David Ellis (ed.): *Fayth*. Elysian Detroit, 2014. (Vol. 3 of *The Oakwood Trilogy*, of which the present book is Vol. 2.)

... and Suffering

Love and suffering have more to do with God than with us. We cannot control suffering caused by natural phenomena. Only God can.

... and Community

Paul was taught by the great rabbis at a time when Judaism had become a religion of measurement: Have you achieved the goals set for you? Paul recognized that human nature leads us to measure ourselves in many different ways to which we cling tightly. Paul was practically drunk with freedom but recognized that most people are not, because they do not know that they can grow with God; that they live and die for God; that no matter what, they are with God. Most people who believe in God measure their closeness to God in increments. If you destroy their belief, they become insecure and might indeed stumble because you are kicking the legs out from under them. It is cruel to destroy people's beliefs—to take away their crutch.

LOVE

You may live in a community but you cannot really participate in it in the way we mundanely mean "participate." At least, I could not. You can only love people, help people, and let them be. God doesn't call you to change the way people think, what they believe. He's just asking us not to hurt others.

God doesn't care whether we know him or not; he only cares about how we live our lives, about how we treat our neighbors. Jesus and Gandhi would not treat the Palestinians the way we do.

There are people who are born ignorant, and they generally live worse lives than those who are not so born. Helpers generally come out of the less ignorant classes, but they are less favored than the ignorant in terms of judgment and grace and mercy. Helping the oppressed is the right thing to do but it still does not raise you above the oppressed.

PRAYER

I HAVE NEVER FELT COMFORTABLE about praying, but I have concluded from our discussions that we should learn from the truly divine snippets of scripture, especially that God's ways are not our ways, and accept that the spirit has to intercede for us with its groanings because we lack the vocabulary to talk to God. But we opt for prayer that makes us feel comfortable. We almost make a religion out of prayer, but the questions we need to ask—the questions God answers—are divine, not religious questions. At the same time, I recognize that any prayer—even prayer that asks God to perform magic—is a good thing if it comforts people in their time of need.

PRAYER

Jesus' prayer in the Garden of Gethsemane was a very human prayer. Something awful was about to happen, and like any of us, he'd have liked it not to. The disciples really didn't know, at that point, what was going to happen. It was late, so it's not surprising they were tired. To be told to stay awake and pray for something they did not comprehend was a bridge too far for them.

Most people pray for a quick end when they know their end is near, or when something bad is happening. We can expect no more than the same outcome Jesus experienced. With faith, we can reach peace.

Praying for wisdom and freedom from fear and want is attractive because if it is granted, then we can start exercising our free will for the common good. When we don't care what happens to us, it is extremely powerful and liberating.

If praying works as so many Christians think, fervently and in good conscience, it can be very toxic, as was demonstrated in recent weeks by the megapastor who was waging war on homosexuality as evil. He attracted huge support through the social media, despite having been fired by the media that broadcast his sermons. His supporters probably took their cue from the surface meaning of these old stories. They did not spend time exploring them in depth.

I recall once discussing with a friend a mutual acquaintance whom I thought of as a good man. My friend said, "Yes, except that he has not accepted Jesus as his lord and savior." Our mutual acquaintance was, in my opinion, hardwired to God, but the label "Jesus" was not pasted on his God. We get into trouble when we try to put labels on God. So if a label for God is X and you don't explicitly acknowledge X as God, then you cannot be hardwired to him—or so my friend's logic went.

When Moses asked God "Who am I to say sent me?" God replied: "Say 'I am' sent you." That is about as explicit a rejection of labeling as one can think of! A label is a definition of the entity to which it is affixed, but God cannot be defined. A

PRAYER

label gives us the illusion that we know what lies beneath it, but in fact the only way to come anywhere close to understanding God is through asking: "Why?" I think God wants us to ask the question, in the same way we want our children to ask "Why?" when we tell them not to put their hands in the fire.

God gave us the ability to ask "Why?" of natural issues, but not of metaphysical issues, not about why bad things happen to good people. Or to me. Prayer is about finding God within us. It is not about changing our environment or circumstances—those are worldly issues we can question, but we must question science, not God, about them. He never answers those questions. For wisdom, we need to find that still, small voice inside us.

Maybe that's the point. God is vague on purpose, because it forces us to ask "Why?"—to search for answers.

Imagine God asking a modern fundamental Christian to save a group of atheist homosexual scientists. The fundamentalist doesn't want grace and mercy for them—he wants punishment and retribution!

To live a life of prayer is to show justice and mercy and humility in the community. To one like me, brought up to believe in prayer but finding it difficult to practice prayer the old-fashioned way, then this is good news. Practicing prayer by contemplating and doing such acts of justice and mercy as I am capable of is something I can do and do gladly.

I don't think I have a relationship with God. I think he has a relationship with me. The idea that we have to follow organized religion robs us of God's promise of justice and mercy for others. God's will is being done and always will be done, regardless of what we think. The assassination of President Kennedy, a random event that could have brought us to nuclear war, made us terribly afraid. It is the randomness of life, its unpredictability, that worries us, so we create religions and ritual and formalized, self-centered prayer to try to ameliorate our fears. Most people want that kind of prayer. They do not want the kind that says I trust God, so let come what may.

It seems to me the gift of prayer was given so that we can center ourselves by establishing a relationship with the principles of God's justice, mercy, righteousness and so on. But we are so far away from practicing the true concept of God's justice, or even from discussing in church such questions as what the cross has to do with justice and what sins the cross cleanses us of. We don't want to confront such questions. We'd rather take the easy route and ask for magic. Yet prayer that centers us to remind us of justice, mercy, and grace is not complex, and has real value.

Isaiah 55:11 seems to support the contention that we don't need to pray:

PRAYER

So will My word be which goes forth from My mouth; It will not return to Me empty, Without accomplishing what I desire, And without succeeding in the matter for which I sent it.

What one prays for has no bearing on the outcome. As Jay just said, it's all about the spirit in which we approach prayer. "Practical" mercy and justice in this life—deliverance from worldly evils such as a tornado, or a Holocaust—can only come from the community, not from God.

When prayer finally removes all my fear, by convincing me that a just, merciful, and gracious God is in ultimate control, then I will be free. It won't matter if there is a Second Coming or not. Nothing will matter, ever again.

A scientist who studies monks has found that more than two hours a day of prayer beneficially re-wires their brains and their thought processes in making them more sensitive and positive with people.

PRAYER

I recall passages in the Old Testament where it seems that God expresses some exasperation that people keep pestering him. It strikes me as unsettling that God would require pestering before he will take action.

To me, prayer is reflection, a quiet time. It is also a holy time: I love ornate Catholic churches; the grander the better. It makes me feel I am in the presence of God and facilitates communication with him. I like the idea of having a holy time (like the Sabbath) or place (a Catholic church) to pray, because in the rush of day-to-day living it is hard to find a holy place and time, so it is hard to pray at all.

I need something that grabs my attention and leads, or even forces, me to be still. An ornate cathedral works. But the drab surroundings of daily life do not encourage or facilitate stillness—prayer—in me. When I am still, it is wonderful, but it does not happen often. Perhaps I need to build a temple in my back yard! Such a place may be just a conduit, a starting point, but it is no less valuable for that reason.

If you do not brush your teeth, you will probably develop cavities. If you do not pray, you may end up hating your Hindu brother-in-law. We can move mountains through prayer. People of all different faiths (and, though they might not admit or realize it, people of non-faith) pray. All that is needed is to focus, to meditate. And when we do, we are all equal in our faith; we are one.

It is easy to see why people would turn atheist when they see ritual prayer in action as during the 2013 massacre at the shopping mall in Kenya. Real prayer can take place anywhere, but it is an intensely personal affair.

The result of prayer is to make the world a better place by loving our neighbors, by preventing the fires of hatred and contempt from consuming the holy bush of compassion and care.

The Gideon story seems far-fetched. I find it hard to believe it was a true story. The reality is that we are all going to die, so why pray for a longer life?

Prayer is more a matter of reflection.

By all means pray if it works for you. I have a basic form of prayer, just talking to him while I am driving to work. It's a far cry from formal prayer, and I have to remind myself to do it, and I have to be in the right frame of mind, but I generally feel better when I do it.

If you measure the results of the Lord's Prayer in "celestial Santa Claus" terms then it would clearly be a fraud. God demonstrably does not give everyone who prays their daily bread, not even those who are really starving. But in the context of Jesus's life and goals, he was driving us to love God and to love our neighbor. God has never been in the business of providing humanity with food and shelter.

The Lord's Prayer is a state of mind, a thought process. I remember being struck, some 15 years ago, by the passage "Be still, and know that I am God" (Psalm 46:10.) The phrase in Romans 8:27: "...and He who searches the hearts knows what the mind of the Spirit is" supports the idea of prayer as a mindset. It's God who searches the heart. It's not a matter of what we say. It's just a recognition that God is doing good things for us, and that we should be doing likewise for our neighbor.

The closest I get to prayer is when I hit upon a quiet spell during a hectic period, and my mind starts to reflect and meditate upon people I love and people I don't love, and maybe that's how God opens my heart to entertain solutions to is-

PRAYER

sues I might be facing. But the subject of prayer, and prayer itself, I find very difficult.

People pray often because they want some bad situation to end or to improve an existing situation. It's human nature. But I do think that some people have the gift of prayer, not in the sense that their prayers tend to get answered but in the sense of having found a way to converse with God. My grandmother was this kind of person. She prayed every night, for up to two hours, for every individual in the family and their unique needs and circumstances. My grandfather told me once that she had prayed deeply for an uncle's safe return from service in WW2. In fact, he did not survive, but during her prayers for him she would feel someone stroking the back of her head. It gave her a sense of peace. That kind of prayer life serves a purpose, if you have that gift. But for most of us, I think just knowing and accepting God's will in our lives gives us what we need.

Matthew 7:7 can be translated from the Greek in two different ways. Jesus was addressing the poor and downtrodden. He is trying to get them to seek a better life, and that takes effort. But we humans prefer to get a better life through magic rather than through effort. And it is this interpretation that the prosperity preachers love. The other way the passage could be translated is "Keep asking, and you will be answered; keep seeking, and you shall find; keep knocking, and the door will be opened." This implies perseverance, and effort.

Would we be disappointed if God did not answer our prayers but instead had given us the ability to solve our own problems?

... and the Parable of the Importunate Widow

I don't see this parable as being about prayer as we know it today. It starts in Luke 17, where Jesus talks about the Second Coming. There are two ways of looking at the story: Either from the perspective of his audience at the time, or from the perspective of a later audience, including ourselves. His audience at the time had other potential Messiahs—not just Jesus—vying for the position. In his writing, the Jewish historian Josephus gave about as much time to John the Baptist as he did to Jesus. To his contemporary audience, he was talking to a people who had been devastated by Rome and whose importunate prayers to be freed from the Roman yoke had fallen on deaf divine ears.

If Jesus were telling the story for the benefit of later generations, such as ours (which is what we assume when we read the Bible) it similarly has no justification in fact.

Importunate prayer failed six million Holocaust victims, along with countless others through the ages. So if the parable as told is to have any meaning, I think it can only refer to the End Time. That is when importunate prayer may get a response. Or maybe not.

... and Forgiveness

Maybe the moving of the mountain is a metaphor for forgiving others. That would make a lot more sense than the notion that God will do anything you want. It's hard—miraculous, perhaps—to be able to forgive.

... and Jacob

Jacob sent his family before him, knowing that they were likely to be slaughtered. He was not concerned, because he thought he could start again on his own. But as it turned out, he needed his family in his disablement.

... and Jonah

The story highlights God's grace. Jonah's prayers try to rob God of his grace, and God is disgusted. The Ninevites worshiped a God that was half-fish, half-man. So they listened to Jonah—who emerged from the belly of a fish—because he seemed like a messenger from their own God. God would not have cared how the Ninevites came to believe in him, he only cared that they *did* believe in him. His mercy shines through this scripture.

PRAYER

Nineveh was extremely violent. God wanted to stop the violence. Not just among the Ninevites but among all Mankind.

Suppose that Jonah had understood God's will. He could have done so much more. He could have stopped wars. But because he would not let go of his self-centered views, this did not happen.

The story of Jonah was written for a Jewish God, but God's genius is that this story (and other Old Testament stories and even the scriptures of other religions) works for—applies to—everybody. God's mercy and grace is, to me, visible in this story.

What was the purpose of the story about Jonah? If it wasn't *about Jonah*, then what? It was about a group of people, the Ninevites, who were persuaded to stop their wicked ways. But we see that historically God does not stop pain and suffering and violence. There's only one way to do that, and that is that through you and me!

I don't think the threat Jonah made to Nineveh was the message God intended. I think he made the threats to goad the Ninevites, but he failed. They listened to God, instead.

... and kingdom

Jesus said that the kingdom is here and now. It is not geographic. It is just a matter of community, but we are unable to create it.

... The Lord's

What a difference it might make in the world if all peoples applied the lesson implicit in "Forgive us our trespasses, as we forgive those who trespass against us". For that to happen, there would need to be mutual understanding, and that alone would be revolutionary. Asking to be "led not into temptation" would mean being asking to be able to understand the other side and to be led to forgive.

The Lord's Prayer is a lesson in how the kingdom community works—through forgiveness and love. In Matthew 22, Jesus said the greatest commandments in the law were to love God, then to love one's neighbor as oneself. This is stated in the Lord's Prayer as: "Forgive us our debts as we forgive our debtors."

... The Children's

Now I lay me down to sleep,
I pray the Lord my soul to keep:
May God guard me through the night
And wake me with the morning light

This prayer used to terrify me as a child. I did not want to think about dying! It must have given me a complex—I have really struggled with prayer ever since.

... of Solomon, Jacob, and Hannah

It is certainly difficult to understand why God would encourage Solomon in his pursuit of the knowledge of good and evil after what he (God) did to Adam and Eve. I tend to agree that the Old Testament in general is problematic, though there are bits I like. I agree that prayer is a force for good and (though he is not visible) that God is involved.

... The High Priestly Prayer

The so-called High Priestly Prayer (John 17) shows that Jesus would support what today we call social welfare. The "comm-unity" of Jesus works because it unites through love of one's fellow human being. Clearly, community through, or of, belief is impossible and has totally escaped us, with our Christians and Moslems and Hindus and Buddhists, and our Protestants and Catholics and Sunni and Shia and…. Our belief system *ought* to be inconsequential compared to our humanity.

... and Gratitude

I do not consider myself the type to pray. It seems to be just not in my personality. I tend to be a negative thinker, especially in the morning. Bothered by my negativity, recently I began a new daily practice of verbalizing my gratitude for the things that seem to deserve it—from my relationships, to the warmth of my car on a cold winter's morning. I do this during my morning commute.

The transformation has been remarkable. I have a new appreciation for life, my anxieties have diminished, my rapport with and ability to manage my staff (whose low education level makes them difficult to communicate with) has improved enormously.

It seems that when one is grateful, one is not influenced by anyone's differences. I find I can live with people and their different ideas when I am grateful for what I have. One simply appreciates the existence of others. Pseudo community wants us to reinforce one another's similar beliefs; gratitude removes this tendency.

The angels ministered to Jesus at the end of his temptation. Since I started practicing gratitude, the angels have been ministering to me, too: Good things have been happening, out of the blue.

... and Fear

If prayer helps you alleviate your fear, that alone is a miracle. Fear is so destructive. And on another matter: Seventh Day Adventist churches[§§] are so plain and boring. Catholic churches, with their rich architecture and iconry, seem to me to be more conducive to putting one in a mood for prayer.

People pray because they are afraid or because they think God wants them to talk to him. Does God really need us to talk to him? No! His message was simply to apply his lessons to one's relationship others.

... and Selfishness

We tend to pray for our own benefit, like Solomon and Jacob and Hannah. We don't necessarily expect a response. But we pray anyway, because it

---

[§§] The church Harry attended all his life.

serves a purpose: It leads us to examine ourselves and our behavior and our motivations.

... and Truth and Love

Mother Theresa exemplifies the fact that theology will never unite us, but love of our fellow human being does. She is loved universally for her selfless charity, not for her religion. Religions are preoccupied with "Truth" rather than with Love. To me, Mother Theresa is the ideal Jesus was asking God for in this prayer.

... and the Inner Light

I have never heard the voice of God and don't think I would like to—it might be too disturbing. But in quite, contemplative times, certain thoughts may resonate with me; thoughts that give me peace, a sense of direction. This what I feel is my communication with God. People who say they have heard the voice of God always want to be followed.

PRAYER

If the inner voice or intuition is the voice of God, then perhaps the communication helps us decide what is right and what is wrong about a situation we are contemplating. The magnificence of Nature does something to us, for sure. It sensitizes us to God, perhaps. It's a kind of prayer.

RELIGION

WHO AM I TO JUDGE whether Jesus is the way or not? The Hindu does not know that Jesus is the way, and it is extremely arrogant of Christians to think that the Hindu should know it!

We can't see God but we want to measure our closeness. Muslims measure their closeness to God by the number of times they pray, and so on. It's not so much about judging than it is about the freedom of knowing that you are God's, no matter what. I eat meat, but I would not bring meat to an Adventist church picnic.***

*** Most Seventh Day Adventists are vegetarians.

RELIGION

Religion generally has been a plague on humanity. Twenty years ago, the feeling among young Adventists was that you had to be an Adventist to go to Heaven.

Christianity, it seems to me, is stunted by the Old Testament. Its stories may yet have some wisdom and truth to offer, but they need to be taken with a grain of salt. The books of the Old Testament were only written down after the second exodus. Before that, they had been transmitted orally for two thousand years, with plenty of opportunity for transmission error and embellishment. This does not prove that the stories are wrong, but it does call for caution in taking them as God's word, as Truth.

Very little of Christian theology comes from the actual teachings of Jesus. Rather, it comes from the comments of Paul. Jesus never speaks of theology or religion. He speaks of healing, mercy, forgiveness, humility.

RELIGION

If you follow the principle he is teaching then you are one with God. It doesn't matter what religion you belong to. If you dissect Christianity, why are there so many sects, so many denominations, when there is only one set of principles?

Jesus used other Gods to get across his message. Jonah, for example, was sent to tell the people of Nineveh that they needed to repent of their wicked ways. Their God was half-fish, half-man. So Jonah was delivered to them via the mouth of a fish—a sign that would be sure to persuade them that he was sent by the God they knew and recognized. So God uses all Gods to get across his message.

Southern conservative religionists have a message that if you don't believe the way they believe then you won't go to heaven. Although these messages have nothing to do with Jesus (who hardly ever spoke of heaven) religions makes a big deal of it. Jesus is about today—how to make this bad world

RELIGION

a better one, how to help those who need help now. Jesus said the kingdom is here now.

The reason religions are so diverse—why there is no single, universal religion—must be that God has not revealed the truth to any of them. I believe that is not his purpose and his will anyway. His will is that we love and care for one another.

Monks meditate in the extreme, but they contribute little to society. It seems to me that it is unnecessary to go to extremes—that there is a middle course, which is to listen to the inner voice telling us that God is there regardless of our religious backgrounds and behavior, as Paul did.

RELIGION

... and Arrogance

The Jews created a process, ceremonies, thinking that made them holy, that it put them on the inside with God.

We should avoid putting ourselves forward as insider sheep. Being a good person is not dependent on following the rules of a religion or on showing oneself to be holy, but on behavior, on unobtrusively helping our fellow man. Those who think they will be first, because they follow the rules, will be last. And *vice versa*.

The parable of the Wandering Sheep transcends culture. We get into trouble when we think it's our culture, or our church, that's keeping us on the straight and narrow and close to God. The message is that God transcends the culture.

The qualities of love, compassion, charity, etc. are common to all humankind. It is arrogant to say that one was chosen by God. The historical and archaeological record shows that the Jewish state was never one of the great civilizations of the Earth. Jesus fought against this arrogance, but it's not unique to Jews. Most religions and sects share this arrogance.

Most scholars accept that the Bible was written over a long and turbulent period of history, during which there was a backlash against the Jews. The robbers and thieves were those who argued "there is only one way and it is through us" — and this is just what the Jewish priests and prophets argued.

... and Fear

The last days of the Roman Empire were brutal. But things eventually got better. Cults in every generation have declared the end to be at hand. We look at that scripture and think Wow! That's us! But the fact is, we have always gotten through such bad times. The scripture is fear-based. Fear is what makes religion grow.

RELIGION

... and Love

The writer of Isaiah [1:11-18] is criticizing his own religion in saying that there are more important things than religious ritual. What's important to God is loving humanity, yet some expressions of love are rejected by religion.

... and Church

I needed the church and its teaching to start my journey. I know it bothers some that I find the church's teaching not pertinent at this point in my journey. But that is not to say that the church was unnecessary in my journey. On the contrary: It was extremely important to me. Without the church's teaching I would not have been able to ask the question "Why do I believe what I do about God?" On the flip side, if I never had the teachings of the church, I might ask myself why I don't believe in anything.

RELIGION

I believe it can be argued that some will search for answers as part of their biological makeup and some find it more secure to accept what has already been established as truth rather than search for answers. Both groups have a purpose. I could not have started my journey unless I belonged to a group that believes it has the answer to what is "truth."

... and Purpose

What is the purpose of the Inner Light? For that matter, what is the purpose of Man? Our lives are about helping others, which leads to a better life for ourselves. Religion, and the Pharisees, care only for control, not about living the truly good life.

... and Worship

Jesus did not ask to be worshipped. The power to do good is of the heart, regardless of one's religion.

RELIGION

... and Science

Since the beginning of human history, humans have sought God, something greater than them that gives peace and hope and love. Most religions founded through the ages have found a God who does offer these things. The ones left standing in modern times war over whose God is the real God, and appeal to their respective scriptures. I think we could apply scientific method to assess these claims of representation and the accompanying dogmatic prescriptions for communion with these Gods, without harming our actual relationship with God at all.

What scares people is to find error in their religious support structure. If I were to find out today that Jesus never rose from the dead, was married, and so on, it would make me extremely uncomfortable but it would not destroy my faith in God! Religion, and the Gods it creates, is not God. Religion's Gods are measurable—their miracles are susceptible to scientific inquiry; the true God cannot be described, let alone measured.

RELIGION

I am not sure if Religion and Science can ever walk in harmony. Religion claims that because its ancient writings were inspired by God, its account of how we got here and where we are going when we die is God's own immutable Truth. Science, in contrast, looks for answers by testing hypotheses through careful experimentation. Religion says its Truth is already complete; Science says we won't know the truth unless we can prove it through testing.

Religion and Science each wants to prove it is right and the other is wrong because both religionists and scientists are fundamentally insecure. They (we!) want to be sure of the purpose and destination of life. Religion claims it already knows, therefore to test and question its beliefs weakens its authority, especially when the answers point to flaws in the ancient writings and beliefs. Religions can only exist with authority when people believe the religion holds absolute truths. Science says truth is not legitimate unless it is tested. Religion wants no part of testing. Ergo, Science and Religion are incompatible.

But Science and *Faith* are not incompatible. They can coexist, in my opinion, because Faith does not depend on absolute truths validated by either ancient scriptures or modern scientific method. Faith is a subjective, feelings-based understanding of a higher power that alone knows the purpose of life. One knows it exists because one can feel it. It is the inner spirit.

...vs. Innocence

John Shelby Spong thinks we should scrap Christianity and start a new religion. Jesus was always surrounded by religious people, but he often walked away from them to mix with unbelievers and sinners. It was as though he too was saying to the religionists that they needed to re-think their religion. It was a profound yet simple message, just like his radical point about becoming like a child. Perhaps all Jesus meant by it is "Start over."

What if we were to encourage newcomers to our church to exhibit the attitude of a child. What would not be important to them would include: How to approach the altar, what songs to sing, whether there should be a drum or no drum. None

RELIGION

of these things that we think are central to our religion and our church are the least bit important, and that is the message Jesus is giving. Certainly, this would induce chaos. But maybe that's the point!

SCRIPTURE

THE MAGIC OF THE BIBLE is that its stories have meaning that can change the heart. It is a pathway to God, despite its contradictions. It is not meant to be taken literally.

What did Jesus want of the disciples? When he said they would all "fall away" because of him, what did he mean? The disciples thought he was the Messiah predicted in Jewish scripture, a real king who would free Israel from bondage. Whose fault is this misunderstanding? Is it Jesus' fault or the disciples' fault? Or is it a fault in translation?

SCRIPTURE

In historical context, the Book of Matthew was written for an historical Jewish audience and is an attack on Judaism. It was telling the Jews that they only looked after their own, whereas God looks after everyone.

The Bible is just one way to listen to God. You may hear Him through other people's experiences. What people are looking for is God's reassurance of peace, of freedom from fear and evil.

The word *Israel* means a people—a nation—that struggles. Over the centuries, Israel the nation has certainly matched that description. Jacob's story troubles me in that God does nothing except to change Jacob's name to Israel. It is a brutal story, and I worry that we try to sanitize and soften it.

SCRIPTURE

It is human nature to be pessimistic. Optimism and forgiveness are hard for us, but when we practice them, we find joy in life. God may well have a hand in all of this but fundamentally it is all down to human nature, not to scriptural "truths." Scripture tries to usurp human nature by breathing *apparent* divinity into it then claiming it as "Truth," as the word of God. Jesus is trying to reverse this. To me, that makes him divine.

The Bible was not given to us ready-made on a golden platter. It has many errors, misspellings, mistranslations, unknowns (including authorship, in most cases), accretions, etc. Its imperfections do not bother me. I regard it as a holy book because it was written for people who are seeking God, and seeking God is a Good thing.

Jesus is asking people to be different. We need to find parallels with today's society. The Bible transcends time—it was written for all ages, albeit in an ancient historical context.

SCRIPTURE

... and Truth

We are searching for truth, understanding, meaning, enlightenment. We all have an inkling that there is a God in charge, and that he is good and merciful, and while I cannot prove it, I draw comfort from it, as the Malays (I am told) derive comfort from their belief in predestination. The important thing is the quest for God. Insight from other faiths would be valuable; but to defend God armed with just the Bible is problematic.

... and Faith

If the Old Testament were all we had to go by, I think there would be far fewer faithful than there are. Luckily, we have Jesus, who came and gave us a completely different message, and a completely different kind of God from the God of Psalms 136 whose "everlasting loving-kindness" did not extend to the Egyptians whose firstborn he massacred to help the Israelites leave. There are bits of value in the Old Testament, but in general its God is not the God of Jesus.

... and Forgiveness and Healing

Where did the Pharisees get the idea of a link between sickness and sin? They got it from Deuteronomy. Jesus took an axe to that link. Who was right: The God of Deuteronomy, or Jesus?

... and Goodness

Goodness is measurable. We can observe and know when it touches someone, unlike "Godheads" and "Truth." And what do we keep going back to, to help us describe and measure goodness?—The Bible! There is nothing wrong in that.

... and the Word

A member of a conservative Baptist church believes that every word of the Bible is true. But if one is grateful for the "message" one can glean from the story, then the details become not significant.

SCRIPTURE

... in Historical Context

We take scripture way out of its original context. The judgment scene was written for clannish agrarian people living in small villages. Jesus was trying to change a way of life. The references in Matthew 25 to hunger, thirst, sickness, etc., were matters of life and death to such people. If you didn't help your neighbor, your neighbor would die. That's not usually the case today. The government will step in, or the missionaries will dig a well for the drought-stricken remote African village. In the time of the Bible, if you were a stranger in a society, you were not entitled to anything. Society then was built around a religion that was exclusive—if you were outside it, you were a stranger, and not deserving of help. So we don't get the full impact of this judgment story in today's context.

The Parable of the Good Samaritan was delivered in the historical context not only of Jewish zealots fighting Roman overlords but also of Jewish priests oppressing and taxing their own people, As a result of all this, many Jews were starving to death.

The priests in the Good Samaritan story do nothing to help the victim. The Samaritan is half-Jewish, half-Arab, yet it is he who does the good deed. So the parable to the audience at the time would have been seen as an appeal to change the religious system.

In asking "Who is my neighbor" the lawyer was probably hoping to hear Jesus reply: "Those who follow the law—the Jews." But of course, Jesus had a very different message. So it was not an "End Time" judgment parable, but a contemporary "judge the Jews" parable.

SHEEP

THE IDENTITY OF ISRAEL has always been tied to being the chosen people. But there were many generations of people before there were ever Jews. Paul is saying nicely to the Jews that the declaration of being God's sole representatives was their declaration, not God's. It seems that Paul himself doesn't fully understand this issue, and he is just awakening to it in this passage in Romans.

... and Goats

In historical context, a more pastoral people knew their sheep from their goats. Verse 31 talks about "all the nations" coming to watch the judgment

SHEEP

and division into sheep and goats. But both goats and sheep have been around forever. They were born what they are. We are what we are, and are going to be what we are going to be.

... and Bible and kingdom

I think we who read the Bible tend to view ourselves as sheep, though not the lost sheep and certainly not the lost coin. But until the Bible was assembled (at about the time of the council of Nicaea in AD 325) one could have no such singular point of view. Before then, with so many disparate communities and books, you might not think of yourself as a sheep of one large flock; but to God, there are no disparities, and he seeks us at his will, not ours.

...Lost

The one sheep that leaves is the only sheep that is found. The 99 are not found. The one lost evidently did not "buy in" to the shepherd. In Luke, he is not put back with the 99, but instead is taken to the shepherd's house for a celebration. It's the 99 who are in trouble, not the one, because the one understands the word of God.

Human nature would be to save the 99 because 99 has much greater value than one, and we would not risk the 99 for the one. So the parable is diametrically opposite to our human inclination and values.

The lost sheep didn't ask to be found. The flock didn't go looking for it. But the sheep had a changed way of thinking—a repentance—when it was found. So the message is that it doesn't matter how far you stray, God will save you.

... Lost from What?

What is the sheep lost from? What is the danger to the sheep? Luke 15 gives more context. At the time it was written, everybody in the audience was a Jew. Jesus was there to tell the poor and disenfranchised—sinners in the eyes of the Pharisees and scribes—that they are not sinners, they are just lost. The passage implies that the other sheep—the Pharisees and scribes—are the real sinners.

... and Religion

There has to be DNA from God inside all of us. All humans have thought, and reason. We are all the same, even though we cluster ourselves, in society and in religion. I chose to believe in a God who loves all of mankind. if God exists for me, if he is intimately involved in my life, then he must be intimately involved in your life and in everyone's life, no matter your or their religion. Similarity on fundamental issues, such as that God is within us all and that we are all expected to be Good, can be found in the scriptures of all the major religions. So it's not a matter of external beliefs imposed on us by, or derived by us from, religion; it is a matter of God's DNA in us.

TRUTH

IF THE NATURAL WORLD is evidence of God's truth then it should be the natural conclusion that the concept of any given truth will change just like the natural world. In nature, nothing stays the same.

Thankfully the world has evolved because of the search for truth. Look back in history and ask yourself would you be comfortable with the supposedly immutable truths of bygone ages? Even though it is painful for mankind to evolve from one truth to another, it is necessary to continue to search for truth for the betterment of Mankind. That is why I believe we continually seek answers. The spirit of God motivates us to ask a question, so it ask can ask us 10 more.

We all believe something; maybe just not an orthodox belief in mainline Christianity or Buddhism or any other system of belief. Many chose an amalgamation of beliefs gathered from religion, philosophy, and science.

Many times we judge what is true not on the basis of what we study but on whom we study. I have a feeling people develop belief systems based on what they see and hear from others. If the mouthpiece is obnoxious or critically outspoken it could move somebody totally away from a system of belief simply because they do not like the mouthpiece it came from and then judge the system from that individual's point of view.

Can we test the Truth that is God? Can we determine whether what the Bible says about God is accurate? Or for that matter whether scripture from any world religion is measurable or accurate? My gut instinct says no. Critical biblical scholars say no. Only those who believe in a religious system tend to believe that what their scripture says is true. In Christianity and Judaism, there are different degrees of what one believes to be true from scripture.

What about people who do not believe in God? Do atheists have the same problem of how to measure that what they believe (that there is no God) is true? My gut instinct tells me they do have the same problem.

Is it ego that pushes us to say openly what we believe to be true? What is wrong with saying "I simply do not know?" We cannot, with historical credibility, attest to who wrote the parts of the Bible or who put them together. Even if we could identify the authors with historical accuracy, how could we know they had the authority to write the word of God? And how could oral stories retold over thousands of years be counted on as giving

TRUTH

accurate accounts of history when simple modern tests have revealed that stories passed around a few people end up significantly corrupted within the span of a single day?

Does the truth matter in the big scheme of life? If so, how? Who benefits? Where did it originate? There are so many questions but there is no irrefutable way to test any answers to such questions for validity, reliability, and accuracy. Yet we argue with passion that our spiritual truth is accurate and complete for the journey of life and community. We shun and ostracize those who do not believe our truths. Why?

What is observable is that humans exhibit tendencies that are good regardless of their religious or non religious backgrounds:

Mercy
Kindness
Selflessness
Compassion
Empathy
Service for the betterment of humanity
Trustworthiness

These human attributes change the world and make it a better place to live. Is it not the goal of a loving God that all his children strive to make their world a better place? My point is that morality and goodness are not exclusive to Christianity or any other religion; they are attributes that humans from all walks and beliefs exhibit. So where do the attributes come from? In my opinion they come from the spirit of God speaking to our hearts.

I did not need to read the 10 Commandments to know that it is better to honor my parents, better not to covet what is not mine, better not to murder or be deceitful or tell untruths for my gain. These laws are built into all of us. They are known by all humanity.

So what is the clarion call to humanity? That is a question only you can answer for yourself.

For me personally these are the truths that I hold on to as being from God. I cannot prove them to you. I cannot say it is the Truth with a capital T. All I can say is that when these truths are applied, the world becomes a better place.

I simply and humbly have to say that I do not know for a fact how God works or how to have a personal relationship with God.

TRUTH

What I can know is that when the attributes I just listed are widespread in our families and communities, then life is better and happier.

The good news is that they exist in every religion and nonreligion, in the hearts of every man and woman. Nobody can take away the truth in your heart.

Those of us who believe in God believe that God is the source of that inner truth, but it doesn't matter what the source was as long as we don't ignore that inner voice in our quest for truth, the meaning of life, and enlightenment.

God's ways are not our ways, and our inability to understand his Word even though we may seek to understand it is immaterial. There are differences in the parable of the Sower and the Seed as it is recorded in three of the synoptic gospels. Mark probably shows the parable in the greatest light in that the way he pens it shows how hard it was to write down.

It seems to me the parable is fundamentally about Jesus himself. He was proclaiming that he is the Word incarnate, and pointing out to the disciples that they had the unique opportunity to see and hear the Word in person.

TRUTH

It's difficult to fit this parable of the Seed to the concept of truth that evolves. Nature changes. But church does offer nuggets of truth.

Soil changes, as the wind blows nutrients onto it (or blows them away). The truth we receive is dependent upon our perception of its source.

Let me play devil's advocate and say that the parable of the Seed is ridiculous, if is saying that soil can choose its nature. The average churchgoing Christian, hearing this parable, would instead assume it means that s/he, the Christian, is the good soil. That is perhaps a judgmental statement, yet I personally perceive it as true. Either way, the parable makes no sense.

There may be events in our lives—a diagnosis of cancer, for example—that turn us rather rapidly into good soil.

The problem for me is that none of the three gospels define what is meant by "the seed" in the parable of the Seed. As devil's advocate, I call the parable "ridiculous" but as Harry I have no problem with it. If it helps you to develop something that is precious to you—love and grace—and share it with everyone then good! But someone else might define the seed as meaning to accept Jesus Christ as one's lord and savior and say that failure to accept the seed dooms one to eternal darkness. So the parable is ridiculous in the sense that it can be made to mean pretty much anything the hearer wants.

We cannot validate the truth of an intangible God. I was raised a Seventh Day Adventist and my source of truth about God was therefore the Bible. It helped shape who I am. But my view of scripture has changed. How else might God communicate his truth with us if not through the Bible? Is the Bible the only way? That would seem to make God pretty small and not very powerful. But scripture itself points repeatedly to another way: Through the heart. I John 4:8-10:

The one who does not love does not know God, for God is love. By this the love of God was manifested in us, that God has sent His only begotten Son into the world so that we might live through Him. In this is love, not that we loved God, but that He loved us and sent His Son to be the propitiation for our sins.

The author of John is saying basically that we don't know God directly so can't love him directly, but God knows us and loves us—that was demonstrated when he sent his son to us. And because of his love for us, he wants us to love one another. Jesus gave us a glimpse of God and God's love for us. Although we cannot truly know and love God, we can know and love those whom we know God loves—each other. That, for me, is the truth. An Adventist missionary's sojourn in Africa to do God's work is an example of God's love put into practice. It is "walking the walk" and worth far more than talking the religious talk. The truth of God is revealed in such instances.

Truth is built into us, in the God spark, the spirit, he puts in all of us. Mark is considered to be one of the oldest gospels, written probably in what is now Italy in about 30 AD. Luke was written some 50 years later. Luke was a physician, fluent in Greek. Luke 1:1-4:

TRUTH

Inasmuch as many have undertaken to compile an account of the things accomplished among us, just as they were handed down to us by those who from the beginning were eyewitnesses and servants of the word, it seemed fitting for me as well, having investigated everything carefully from the beginning, to write it out for you in consecutive order, most excellent Theophilus; so that you may know the exact truth about the things you have been taught.

The paradox is that early church fathers used Mark as their basis for truth. Luke would have had access to Mark's gospel. Why did he not just take Mark as the gospel truth? Did he not find the truth there? His gospel is somewhat different. Why do we have so many slightly different accounts? My point is that even back then, the authors of the New Testament were searching for truth in a story they thought was special and mystical. To me, that is what makes their writing divine. That there are historical errors and differences is irrelevant. What matters is that they help in the search for divine truth. The proof of that statement can be deduced from the fact that for 2,000 years the gospels have been, and remain to this day, the most powerful source of divine truth, though not necessarily of precise historical truth, for millions of people.

TRUTH

What if we decide that our group has discovered "the Truth"? If we, or any one of us, thinks we know it, are we then bound to share it with others? Isn't Truth a matter for the individual? All religions share millions of small-t truths that may help the individual find capital-T Truth. But it is impossible to express the Truth in words.

We all know what is the right thing to do. The problem is that the right thing to do often crosses or ignores religious lines and boundaries. It may run counter to someone's interpretation of scripture. For that reason, religions fear the truth, because it may undermine their reason for being. There would be no purpose in meeting to share the truth with others. There would be no reason for different denominations. There would be no meaningful distinction between believer and nonbeliever.

We should not define ourselves by the Bible. We should be defined by our inner light. That is not to

TRUTH

say that we should not meet to study the Bible. At all of our meetings (and today has been no exception) we are each more or less enlightened by some Bible passage or other. But the only visible truth is how we treat others, how we share grace and love.

I think there is a big, capital T, Truth in the Bible. I think it is selfless love, as exemplified by Jesus. But the problem is that we tend to capitalize the t of the small truths. We quickly fail at selfless love when others challenge our truths. We can't prove the existence of God, but we all can point to something that resonates inside us, the greater Truth that point to his existence.

... and Faith

I can agree on one thing with people of faith: That faith is the bridge to belief. But faith and belief do not always equal the truth.

... and Love

Everyone responds to love, even atheists. But not everyone responds to Truth. It is difficult to pass on the Truth, but it is not so difficult to love. That is an easy answer, but it is also an answer to spreading Truth! People come to blows over perceptions of Truth, but there is no violence in a loving interaction. Nobody in his or her right mind argues against the definition or the existence or the benefits of love, yet will argue the blazes over the definition and existence of Truth.

So to me, the path to enlightenment is through love, not so much Truth.

... and Mystery

Exodus 3:14: God said to Moses, "I am who I am" (or "I will be what I will be"). "This is what you are to say to the Israelites: 'I am has sent me to you.'" In other words, God is a mystery. We know nothing about him except what Jesus has taught us.

John 8:53-58 suggests that "I Am-ness" is should be in all of us:

TRUTH

Are you greater than our father Abraham? He died, and so did the prophets. Who do you think you are?"

Jesus replied, "If I glorify myself, my glory means nothing. My Father, whom you claim as your God, is the one who glorifies me. Though you do not know him, I know him. If I said I did not, I would be a liar like you, but I do know him and obey his word. Your father Abraham rejoiced at the thought of seeing my day; he saw it and was glad."

"You are not yet fifty years old," they said to him, "and you have seen Abraham!"

"Very truly I tell you," Jesus answered, "before Abraham was born, I am!"

... and Prayer

"Ask God a question and he will ask you ten questions in return." To me, the moral of that insight is that God is not in the business of answering questions. It is we who are in the business of answering questions and shaping our thoughts to establish truths for our community, even though the truths we establish will be challenged and change over time. To some this is very unsettling and contrary to the concept of truth. One aspect of truth never changes though: Established ideas, taken to be true, change over the timeline of history. As Franklin D. Roosevelt might have put: Nothing is permanent except change itself!

... and Science and Religion

Can religion borrow from science a way to test its "immutable" truths? Religious truths—by which I mean dogmatic truths, scriptures, the Bible—evolve and change also. They do not affect the ultimate truths we all carry within us with the inner light, but to the extent they are touted as immutable then they are open to exposure, by science, as mutable and impermanent. Religion can put its dogmas to scientific test without risk to faith. The risk (which is not a risk) would be that religion itself might have to change.

POTPOURRI

Emptiness

Jesus was grateful for his relationship with God, so he did not need to succumb to the temptation of possessions, and in the end, he received his reward for emptying himself, in the form of the kingdom of heaven.

Daoism

I AM OK Doing Nothing for the first half hour in the morning, but after that, the feeling dissipates.

Temptation

DARKNESS is easier to embrace than light.

The Devil tempted Jesus to show his divinity during his 40 days and nights in the desert, by turning stones into bread and by leaping off a cliff. His rejection of the temptation seems almost a reprimand to the Israelites for not learning from *their* 40 years in the desert. Canaan was a bountiful land of milk and honey, but the Israelites ruined it every time they entered it.

Beatitudes

THE BIGGEST PROBLEM God ever had was when Adam and Eve ate of the forbidden fruit. His promise that he was the way forward covered for them; they didn't (and we don't) need knowledge.

POTPOURRI

Every one of us will at some point in our lives need a Beatitudinal blessing; all God is saying is when that time comes, don't worry about it—you *will* be blessed!

Are the Beatitudes an à la carte menu? Must we choose between either being rich in spirit or seeing God? The more we read the Bible, the more we seem to see a pathway being delineated for us.

Innocence

CHILDREN DEPEND on adults, though they don't necessarily know it. To them, the world just is what it is. They get hungry, and food appears before them. Children don't spend time worrying about much at all. They just go about enjoying life.

Some of the nicest people I know are just like children. They simply enjoy life. That is their way, and perhaps it is the way to the kingdom. So perhaps we should not be concerned with finding the way but instead should just follow the way we are already on!

In the Old Testament, you get the sense that God doesn't want us to know who he is. Perhaps innocence of knowledge of God, as a child would possess, is what we should strive for.

Judgment and the Parable of the Wheat and the Tares

THE DEVIL who planted the tares in the parable of the Wheat and the Tares was not a fallen angel at the time of Jesus. Lucifer fell several hundred years later, around the time of Constantine. So who was causing the problems with the tares? If you don't know who the enemy is, and if wheat and tares are hard to distinguish one from the other, how can we know what to do?

POTPOURRI

EPITAPH

"I love all of yous, irregardless."

—Harry Tompkins

*Harry was fluent in speech
and a better writer
than he gave himself credit for.
He had two quirks of vocabulary
that further endeared him to us in life.
Put together in the sentence above,
they epitomize the man.*

www.ingramcontent.com/pod-product-compliance
Lightning Source LLC
Chambersburg PA
CBHW031444040426
42444CB00007B/969